All You Wanted To Know About
Family Planning

DR. D.N. KAKAR

New Dawn

NEW DAWN
An imprint of Sterling Publishers (P) Ltd.
A-59, Okhla Indl. Area, Phase-II, New Delhi-110020
Ph.: 6313023, 6916209, 6916165 Fax: 91-11-6190028
E-mail: ghai@nde.vsnl.net.in
http://www.sterlingpublishers.com

All You Wanted To Know About Family Planning
©2001, Sterling Publishers Private Limited
ISBN 9788120794627

All rights are reserved. No part of this publication may be
reproduced, stored in a retrieval system or transmitted, in any form
or by any means, mechanical, photocopying, recording or
otherwise, without prior written permission of the publisher.

Published by Sterling Publishers Pvt. Ltd., New Delhi-110020.
Lasertypeset by Vikas Compographics, New Delhi-110020.
Printed at Prolific Incorporated, New Delhi-110020.

Preface

All you wanted to know about family planning is an easy-to-understand reference series put together for your convenience. The material presented is based on a review of current literature, including various reports of the World Health Organization, resource books, population reports and scientific papers. The update is intended to enhance your knowledge about family planning and to help you adopt appropriate methods of family planning. Care is taken to present factual information in a straight-forward manner. The sole purpose of the book is to help individuals make informed choices about family planning.

Dr. D.N. Kakar
President
The Environment Society of Haryana

Contents

Preface		3
Introduction		6
1.	Natural Methods of Family Planning	9
2.	Barrier Methods of Contraception	30
3.	Intrauterine Contraceptive Devices	60
4.	Injectable Contraceptives and Norplant Implants	88
5.	Oral Contraceptives	115
6.	Sterilisation	144
7.	Other Methods of Family Planning	186

Introduction

Appropriate use of any form of contraception should be based on information, education and communication (IEC). Users must have access to correct information about contraceptive methods for making informed choices from the methods available. They must know how the methods work and their contraindications, advantages and disadvantages. They must also know, how to manage their method-related problems with the help of service providers. The information provided here is meant to enhance the knowledge of potential users about different methods of family planning. The user who has made an informed choice of a particular contraceptive method is more likely to feel satisfied with it. Ultimately he or she can be a potential promoter of that method of family planning.

Family planning methods over the past twenty-five years have been developed mainly for the female reproductive system. It was assumed that women have greater motivation to take control of their reproductive destiny. After all, it is the woman who undergoes pregnancy, gives birth, nurses, and has greater overall responsibility of raising the child. Ideally both parents must take a joint decision as to the method they would like to adopt, after careful consideration of options that would suit them best. For an intelligent and satisfying decision, it is necessary to be well informed of the implication of each option.

Natural Methods of Family Planning

What is family planning?
Planning helps to achieve better results in the most economic, least problematic and most satisfactory manner. Family planning means to plan a family in such a manner that there is all-round growth and development of the family as a whole and individuals in it. A well planned family has emotional and all forms of stability. There is happiness and progress.

Why do you need to know about family planning?

You need to know about family planning, because it will help you to manage your family and your life better. Throughout the world it has already helped millions of people in many ways. It has helped in saving women's lives. With contraception, many women have succeeded in avoiding unsafe abortions and unintended pregnancies. Many women have been able to manipulate births to their healthiest child bearing years. Family planning programmes have also helped in saving children's lives. It has helped women to space pregnancies and to have healthier children. Today, family planning programmes offer many choices. Many women have succeeded in controlling childbearing by using effective contraception. There is no doubt that couples with fewer children are better equipped to provide good education to their offsprings. Now, in the face of HIV/AIDS, sexually active people need to protect themselves against sexually transmitted diseases. Family planning programmes have encouraged the use of condoms, as well as the correct use of condoms, and sex only in monogamous relationships.

What are the various types of contraceptive methods?

There are many types of contraceptive methods: for males, females, or for both as well as temporary and permanent ones. The *temporary methods* are classified as:
1. behavioral (abstinence, rhythm method, coitus interruptus);
2. barrier methods (mechanical: male-condom, female-diaphragm, cervical cap, vault cap, vimule);
3. chemical (spermicides);

4. combined (mechanical plus chemical);
5. intrauterine contraceptive devices (IUCD);
6. hormonal (combination pills), injectables; implants, vaginal rings and hormonal releasing IUCD);
7. utertuberal junction devices;
8. immunological;
9. interceptive; and
10. post-conception medical termination of pregnancy.

Permanent methods comprise female sterilisation and male sterilisation.

You will appreciate that if more people choose family planning, fertility will fall and population growth will also slow down. This will be of tremendous help in conserving resources and improving health. Hopefully, the provision of information about family planning in an easy-to-understand manner will help many young people in making sexual decisions responsibly and avoiding sexually transmitted diseases as well as unintended pregnancies.

What is Natural Family Planning?
Natural Family Planning (NFP) is a term which describes methods of

planning, delaying or preventing pregnancies without using any artificial means. The male NFP method means the withdrawal of the pennis just before ejaculation. In females, NFP is based on observation of naturally occurring signs and symptoms of the fertile and infertile phases of the menstrual cycle. A large number of people have been benefitted by NFP. They have succeeded in avoiding or delaying pregnancies by abstaining from intercourse on potentially fertile days. But people wanting to use NFP should be able to identify the fertile and infertile phases of the menstrual cycle. In fact, NFP is a technique for determining the fertile period. It is not a method of contraception. Techniques used include the Rhythm or Calendar Method Basal Body Temperature Method and the Cervical Mucus (a Bilings) Method and the Coitus Interruptus.

What are the advantages & disadvantages of NFP?

Advantages

- Absence of any physical side-effects;
- Greater awareness and knowledge of human reproductive functions;

- Development of self-reliance;
- Promotion of shared responsibility of the couple for family planning; and
- Its usage is not dependent on medically qualified personnel.

Disadvantages
- The requirement of commitment and cooperation of both partners;
- The requirement of daily records of signs of fertility by the users;
- The requirement of a trained NFP teacher for explaining the techniques; and
- Possibility of emotional stress in some cases, as a result of the

need to abstain from intercourse between 8 and 16 days.

Explain the different techniques of NFP

I Rhythm or Calender Method

The Rhythm or Calendar method is based on the fact that ovulation occurs about two weeks before menstruation, regardless of the length of a woman's menstrual cycle. At best, this method can provide a rough estimate of the fertile time. One has to calculate a woman's fertile phase (unsafe period) from the records of her menstrual cycle of the previous six months to twelve months, taking into consideration her shortest and longest cycle. For instance, if a woman's menstrual cycle shows that her shortest cycle was of twenty-five days and her longest cycle was of thirty-one days, her first fertile day will be the 7th day of her cycle (25 to 18) and her last fertile day will be the 20th day of her cycle (31 to 11).

There are various formulae to calculate the fertile days in the cycle. For example, if the record of the cycle length for six months varies from 25, 28, 26, 30, 26, 28 days, then, first substract 20 days from the shortest cycle to calculate the first fertile day and then substract 10 days from the longest cycle to calculate the last fertile day. The fertile phase then will be from day five to day 20 (30-10 - unsafe period). Thus one has to observe abstinence from day five to day twenty (both days inclusive). The biggest advantage is that awareness of the fertile phase and the infertile phase of the menstrual cycle can help a couple in decision-making about avoidance of pregnancy. But the main disadvantage is that this method provides a very rough estimate of the fertile phase and a woman has to be very alert in keeping a record of her menstrual cycle for 6 to 12 months.

Basal Body Temperature Method

This method is based on the fact that progesterone from the corpus luteum raises the temperature of the body at complete rest by 0.2 and 0.4°C and maintains it at this level until the onset of the next menstruation. But this method is functional only when concrete instructions are followed for taking the temperature. The user is instructed to use a special ovulation thermometer graduated from 36-38°C. However, the user must record the temperature at the same time each day immediately after working or before eating or drinking. The user must keep the thermometer in the mouth for five minutes. The temperature should be recorded on the chart in the centre of the appropriate square. The user is instructed to begin a new chart on the first day of the menstrual period. The main difficulty with this method is that sometimes it is difficult to interpret the charts. The infertile phase begins as soon as records show a rise in body temperature for 3 consecutive days as compared to the previous six consecutive days (excluding days 1-4 of the cycle). The user can have unprotected intercourse from the 3rd day of temperature rise until the beginning of the next menstrual period.

Ovulation Method (Cervical Mucus or Billing's Method)

This method is based on recognising the changes that occur in the cervical mucus under the influence of oestrogen and progestren at different times in the menstrual cycle. The user can recognise four phases: ● the dry days following menstruation; ● the days in the early pre-ovulatory phase when the mucus first appears; and ● the wet days immediately prior to ovulation and the days following the peak during which the mucus becomes sticky and scanty. Here again the user is instructed to make observations each day on an appropriate chart, by using certain identification marks such as P for periods, D for dry, M for moist, etc. The user is instructed to have intercourse on alternate dry days following menstruation. Otherwise, the couple must abstain from sexual intercourse. In fact, sexual intercourse should be avoided until the evening of the fourth day after the peak mucus.

The user should clearly understand that the effectiveness of natural family planning methods depends on a variety of factors such as ● the fertility indicators used; ● the validity of the rules used; ● the type and quality of teaching; ● the ability of the woman to observe and interpret her fertility signs; ● the ability of the couple to abstain from vaginal intercourse; and ● certain characteristics of the couple, including the woman's history of pelvic infection. All women in different stages of their reproductive life can use natural family planning. Even a woman with irregular cycles can use NFP. And there are no risks or harmful effects of using this method. In fact, NFP can be combined with other methods. But pre-menopausal women and women who have undergone cervical surgery may experience some difficulty in adopting natural family planning methods. However, a partner's unwillingness to observe periodic abstinence can affect the use of natural family planning methods. Obviously, high motivation is required for effective use of these methods.

Coitus Interruptus Method

Coitus interruptus is one of the oldest methods of birth control, widely used in many communities. Basically, coitus interruptus is withdrawal of the erect penis from the vagina before ejaculation. Thus, ejaculation into the vagina or even on the external genitals of the woman is avoided. Since ejaculation occurs outside the vagina, semen is not deposited within the vagina and pregnancy is avoided. The failure rate of the method is 5 to 25 pregnancies per 100 couple years. The failure rates vary with the age and experience of the couple. But there are some other reasons for its failure, including: premature ejaculation, ejaculation into the vagina due to failure to withdraw the penis in time, ejaculation on the vulva and pre-ejaculatory emission which often contains some spermatozoa which can fertilize an ovum. However, this method may not provide total enjoyment to the couple. Yet there are certain advantages of this method: ● no equipment or preparation is required; ● it is free from medical supervision or follow-up; ● it costs nothing; ● it is free from psychological or physical side-effects; and

- it allows total privacy to the couple's sexual relationship. This method is widely practised in the Philippines (26%), Hungary (23%), Jordan (13%), and Colombia (10%). In developing countries, the proportion of married women, aged 15-29 years, who rely on this method, is twice the proportion of all married women. This method is utilised by women as a transition method, i.e. before accepting the intrauterine device (IUD) or oral contraceptives.

Barrier Methods of Contraception

What are the barrier methods of contraception?

Basically, barrier methods of contraception involve the use of things that prevent conception by either mechanical or chemical means or both. These methods include: condoms, diaphragms, cervical caps, spermicides (foams tablets, creams and jellies) and sponges. For optimum efficacy, one should have a clear understanding of these methods.

What are condoms ?

Condoms or sheaths are usually made of rubber and they prevent sperms from getting into the vagina. As you know, the condom is one of the oldest and most commonly used methods of contraception. Earlier, it was used mainly for the prevention of sexually transmitted diseases but now it is increasingly being used for contraception. The word 'condom' has its origin in the Greek word 'condus', but is derived from the original Persian word 'Kendu' which means a long storage vessel made from animal intestine. In the

18th century, condoms were made from animal caeca. In 1901, a condom with a teat was developed. But in the early 1930s, latex rubber was used to manufacture condoms. Dry lubricated condoms were developed in the 1960's by using silicon which provided greater sensitivity during coitus. The average condom is about 19 cm long and 2.5 cm wide, is lubricated and is of a dull tan colour. Certain brands of condoms also contain spermicide nonoxynol - 9 with the lubricant. The spermicide is distributed with the lubricant over both the inner and outer surface of the condom. Lubricated condoms can enhance sexual pleasure because they can reduce mechanical friction and irritation of the penis or the vagina.

You may like to know that a decade ago, about 6,000 million condoms were used each year and 45 million married couples were relying on condoms. Nearly 60 per cent of married condom users are in developed countries. In Japan, about 50 per cent of married couples rely on condoms for family planning and in Finland, Sweden, Denmark and Scandinavia nearly 20 per cent married couples rely on condoms. The situation is different in developing countries where only 4 per cent of married couples of reproductive age use condoms for family planning. In India, 14 per cent of married couples using family planning methods rely on condoms. There has been an increase in the use of condoms in response to AIDS, but it is not yet clear how much of this use is within marriage and how much outside marriage.

In India, condoms (Nirodh) are available almost free of cost at various government family welfare centres and at centres run by various voluntary health agencies. Condoms are also available at a chemist's in rural and in urban areas. The correct and consistent use of a condom has the advantage of safeguarding not only against pregnancy but also against sexually transmitted diseases and HIV/AIDS. A condom is put on the male organ before intercourse, holding its tip and releasing the air. One must carefully unroll it over the erect organ. One must ensure that the outer rim is outside when the condom is unrolled. One must also ensure its safe withdrawal from within the vagina. And the condom should be disposed off by tying a knot near its open end. A new condom should be used for each intercourse. It has been reported that re-use of a condom is associated with high breakage rates. Latex membranes are generally not strong enough to withstand repeated stretching, friction and cleaning. The latex condoms should not be used with oil-based lubricants or products. Some vaginal creams (Monistat, Estrace, Femstat, Vagisil and Premarin), vaginal spermicides (Rendell's Cone and Pharmatex Ovule) and sexual lubricants

(Elbow Grease, Hot Elbow Grease and Shaft) should not be used as these products weaken the latex condoms. Only water-based products should be used as these have not yet shown any harmful effects.

What are the advantages and disadvantages of condoms?

Regarding their advantages, most condoms can be used on a long-term basis without any side-effects or health hazards. There are no contraindications. Condoms are easily available without prescription. Condoms are also more self-explanatory than some other methods. Moreover, the male is involved in contraceptive decision-making. They are suitable for those couples who do not find other methods, such as IUCD, pills or injectables, suitable. Condoms also provide protection against pelvic inflammatory diseases to women. Besides, pregnant women are provided protection against amniotic infections when condoms are used.

Regarding the disadvantages of condoms, some users may complain of reduction in sexual pleasure because of lack of genital contact, while others may consider condoms as 'messy'. Besides, condoms can get torn by a fingernail or other sharp objects. That is why condoms are not as effective as other methods of contraception, like the IUCD and pills. In some cultures, condoms are associated with illicit sexual activities. Some users may also be allergic to rubber. In any case, male cooperation is needed for using condoms and this may be a disadvantage in some circumstances. Regarding their effectiveness, condoms can be nearly as effective as other methods if used properly. Pregnancy rates among condom users are reported to be 0.6 to 6.8 per 100 couple years. Breakage rates, ranging from less than 1 to 12 per 100 vaginal intercourses have been reported in prospective studies. However, these rates are dependent on • sexual behaviour and practices • experience with using condoms; • use of lubricants; and • improper storage.

How effective is a condom as a family planning method? Can it prevent sexually transmitted diseases?

If used correctly, every time the user has sex, the condom is indeed an effective family planning method. Condoms also provide protection against sexually transmitted diseases including HIV/AIDS. Some users may find condoms helpful in keeping an erection longer. Even sexual intercourse and the pleasure before ejaculation may be of a longer duration.

How can a woman persuade her husband to use a condom or insist on his using one?

She can bring to his notice that the correct use of condoms can make sex enjoyable, prevent sexually transmitted diseases, including

HIV/AIDS, besides preventing pregnancy and serious illness.

What can be done to avoid the breaking of condoms during sex?

Normally, if condoms are correctly used, they will seldom break. However, a condom could break if a woman's vagina is dry. This can be remedied by using a water-based lubricant. Prolonged foreplay before sex may often make a woman's vagina wetter. However, under no circumstances, should one resort to using any oil or lubricant such as petroleum jelly or a skin cream. These can lead to breaking of condoms by weakening the latex rubber. Also, a woman must ensure that her husband uses a condom even when he wants to have oral or anal sex.

What are diaphragms?

The diaphragm is a dome-shaped rubber cup with a flexible rim. It is inserted into the vagina in such a way that the posterior rim rests in the posterior fornix and the anterior rim fits snugly behind the pubic bone. The dome of the diaphragm covers the cervix and the spermicidal cream or jelly placed in the dome before insertion, is held in contact with the surface of the cervix. The contraceptive effect of the diaphragm depends partly on its function as a barrier, decreasing the degree of contact between the semen and the cervix and partly on its function as a spermicide holder. (Figure 1)

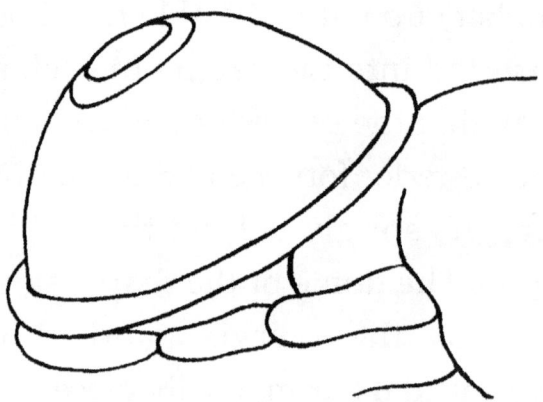

Fig. 1 Diaphragm

What are the advantages and disadvantages of using a diaphragm?

Regarding its advantages, the diaphragm is safe and effective, if used correctly. Its use is not dependent on the male. Moreover, it includes both barrier and spermicidal mechanisms of action. It also makes a woman aware of her reproductive anatomy. Regarding its disadvantages, the diaphragm is fairly expensive and requires fitting by a clinician or a trained person. Again, as it is large and conspicuous, some women have difficulty in removing it. It can even get dislodged before or during intercourse and it requires washing and proper storage. Besides, its incorrect use may limit its effectiveness. Moreover, the diaphragm can also interrupt intercourse, if not inserted in advance. The user should insert it any time up to six hours before intercourse. She must put contraceptive jelly or cream into the diaphragm. For this, she should hold the diaphragm with the dome down and the rim up - just like a cup and should avoid using vaseline or other petroleum products because of their damaging effect. Before inserting a diaphragm, the cervix must be located with the finger. She must ensure that the cervix is covered by the soft rubber dome of the diaphragm and that the front rim is snugly in place behind the pubic bone. After intercourse, the diaphragm should be left in place for at least six hours, and after removal, should be washed with mild soap, rinsed with water, and then dried with a towel. One should avoid using talcum or perfumed powder on the diaphragm. Use of a diaphragm should also be avoided during a menstrual period. The user should check the fit of her diaphragm if she loses more than four kgs of weight, if her diaphragm causes discomfort or pain, if she had a pelvic surgery or if she feels that her diaphragm is too loose or too small. There are certain side-effects/complications, such as allergic reactions to rubber (latex) or the spermicidal agent and monilial vaginitis, if the diaphragm is not well cleaned and dried before re-use.

The diaphragm and the spermicide combination may also confer some protection against sexually transmitted diseases. Besides, the diaphragm may also have some protective effect against cervical dysplasia (a pre-cancerous condition).

What are cervical caps and what are their advantages and disadvantages?

There are three types of cervical caps: the Cavity rim cap (cervical cap), the Vimule cap, and the Vault cap. All of these are made of latex rubber. But their use is limited to a few countries, such as Australia, NewZealand, UK and the US. The Cavity rim cap is a thimble shaped cap which is available in four sizes with inside diameters of 22, 25, 28, 31 mm respectively. This cap covers the length of the cervix. This cap is in general use. The Vimule cap is belt shaped and is available in three sizes with outside diameters of 42, 48 and 52 mm respectively. This cap is particularly suitable if the cervix is irregular, short or too large for the largest cavity rim device. The Vault cap is bowl shaped and is available in five sizes ranging from 50 to 70 mm (outside diameter). It is made of heavier material than that of the diaphragm. The advantages of the cervical cap are that it appears to be safe; quite effective if used correctly — uses both barrier and spermicidal mechanisms of action; is less messy, its use is not dependent on the male;

and it makes a woman aware of her reproductive anatomy. But the disadvantages are, that the fitting of a cap requires a specially trained person; the cap may get dislodged; it may cause abrasion or laceration of the vaginal walls and the cervix; it is fairly expensive; intercourse may be interrupted; and vaginal manipulation may be discouraged in some cultural settings. (Figure 2, 3, 4)

Fig. 2 Cavity Cap

Fig. 3 Vimule Cap

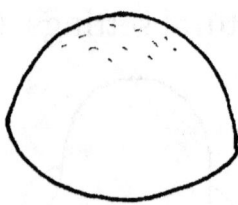

Fig. 4 Vault Cap (Dumax)

Which women can use the cervical cap?

Women with any number of children can use the cervical cap but parous women tend to have a much higher pregnancy rate than nulliparous women. After delivery, women should wait for at least six weeks before using the cervical cap. Even a woman undergoing an abortion should wait for 4 to 6 weeks before deciding to use the cervical cap. It takes 4 to 6 weeks for the uterine involution to be complete and bleeding/spotting can continue for eight weeks. The use of the cervical cap is contraindicated during bleeding. The cervical cap should not be removed before 6-8 hours after intercourse.

What are sponges and what are their advantages and disadvantages?

The contraceptive sponge is a soft, disposable, polyurethane sponge, containing enough spermicides to last 24 hours. The sponge operates in three ways: it forms a physical barrier between the sperm and the cervix, it contains a spermicide that kills sperms on contact, and it traps and absorb the sperms. The advantages of the sponge are, that it is safe if used correctly, it is easy to insert, it uses both barrier and spermicide mechanisms of action, its use is not dependent on the male, it absorbs semen and it is easily available. However, it makes a woman more aware of her reproductive anatomy. But the disadvantages are that it occasionally causes irritation. Some women may find it difficult to remove it or insert it and may even forget to remove it. Moreover, it may become dislodged and cause interruption of sexual intercourse if the sponge is not inserted in advance. The user should wet the sponge with clean water and also squeeze the sponge gently to remove excess water. She should avoid using a dry sponge and before inserting the sponge should locate the cervix with the finger. After insertion, she should check again to ensure that the cervix is still covered by the sponge. She should wait for six hours after the last act of intercourse before removing the sponge and should avoid leaving the sponge in place for more than 24 hours. Sponge should be removed gently to avoid tearing. And, she should not use the sponge when she is having menstrual bleeding.

What are spermicides and what are their advantages and disadvantages?

Spermicides are chemical agents that inactivate the sperms in the vagina before they can move into the upper genital tract. The spermicidal agents used in most spermicides are surfactants - surface active compounds that destroy the sperm cell membranes. Currently, there are nine forms of spermicide carriers; jellies (gel); creams; foams (aerosols); melting suppositories; soluble films; condom lubricants; and sponges. The main advantages of spermicides are that they are safe, fairly effective if used consistently and correctly and are easily avialable without any prescription. Moreover, the use of spermicides is not dependent on the decision of the male partner. It is also easy to transport, as it is wrapped in a foil and it is not affected by heat or moisture.

Regarding its disadvantages, some users may find it messy and it may even produce vaginal irritation or allergic reaction. Sexual intercourse may need to be interrupted and may decrease the sexual enjoyment. Foaming tablets, suppositories and foam may also release heat and vaginal discharge. Some of the non-contraceptive benefits of spermicides include: prevention of sexually transmitted diseases, prevention of upper genital tract infection (PID), and protection against cervical neoplasia. The users of spermicidal creams and gels may have intercourse as soon as the cream or gel has been introduced. But the users of spermicidal tablets and suppositories should wait for 1-30 minutes after insertion of the tablet in the vagina for proper dissolving of the tablet. Spermicide is not effective if it is not dissolved properly.

Intrauterine Contraceptive Devices

What is an Intrauterine Contraceptive Device (IUCD/IUD)? How was it developed?

An Intrauterine Contraceptive Device (IUCD) is worn by the female in the uterine cavity. She can get it inserted by a trained doctor or a paramedical. For more than 70 years, IUCDs in some form or other have served a useful purpose as a realistic method of contraception.

No doubt its development took place at a slow pace. One cannot forget the use of wishbone and collar stud pessaries of the 19th century and of course, Richter, Grafenberg and Ota rings of the earlier 20th century. In the 1960s, there were silastic devices, which were available in a wide variety of plastic shapes. In the 1970s, there were copper IUDs, which had copper wire wound around silastic frames. But it was in the late 1970s that we witnessed the development of second generation copper devices with sleeves of copper, instead of copper wire, to prolong its active life. In fact, by now, many different shapes of IUDs are available. The purpose is to reduce the risk of expulsion. Some hormone-releasing medicated devices were also developed. These contain progesterone or levonorgestrel.

It was Richard Richter who in 1909 described a practical intrauterine device for the first time. He described the use of a flexible ring of silkworm gut which could be placed in the uteri of a woman seeking contraceptive help. Then, after a gap of two decades, Grafenberg, in 1929, re-emphasised the use of a contraceptive device, wholly within the uterus. He was able to draw the attention of gynaecologists through his work with an IUD, first made of silkworm gut and later of silver wire. People had already started fitting devices of one sort or another during this period. Hall in America, Jackson in England and Knoch in Indonesia, were fitting these devices, while Ota in Japan was using a modified Grafenberg ring since 1934. However, the year 1959, witnessed further developments with various types of IUCDs. And the credit for this goes to Oppenheimer who spent about two decades developing these IUCDs. These events led to the holding of the First International Conference on IUCD in New York, in 1962. Subsequently, Tietze, in 1963, set up the Co-operative Statistical Program for the Evaluation of Contraceptive Devices (CSP). In the late 1960s, usual copper devices were available.

Name the different types of IUCD's that are currently available.

Currently, the available devices can be divided into three categories: inert or plastic; • copper; and • medicated. Each one of these has one or two threads attached to it. Their identification becomes easy through the colour of their thread.

Inert Devices: These are plain silastic devices made in different shapes and sizes. Many of them contain barium sulphate to make them radio-opaque. However, the most popular one is Lippes loop and is available in many countries in different shapes and sizes (Fig. 6).

Copper Devices: The most currently available copper devices contain copper which helps in increasing the contraceptive efficacy. These devices are smaller and easier to fit.

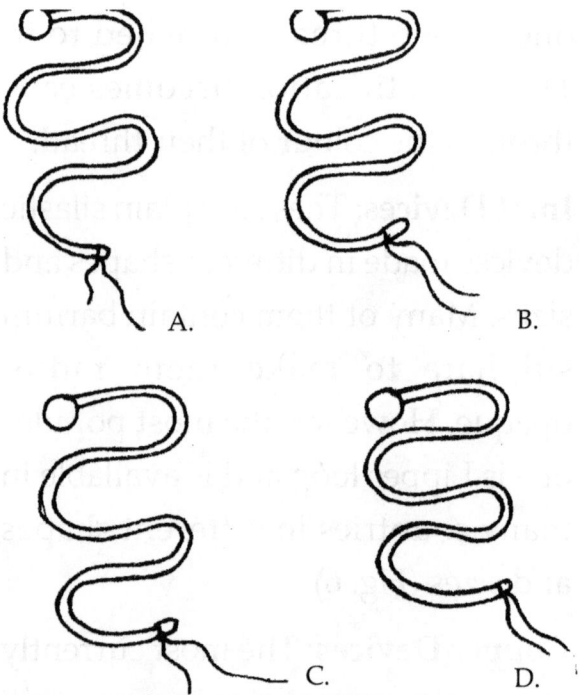

Fig. 6 Types of Lippes Loop

Commonly used copper devices include Tcu-380, the Cu-220C, the Nova T and the Multiload - 375 (ML

Cu-375). Currently, Copper T model T 220C is widely used in the family planning programme.

CuT200 : This device is T-shaped, made of polyethylene and is 36 mm long and 32 mm wide. It releases copper at the rate of 50 mcg per day. After three years of use, the rate of release of copper is known to decrease, so its effective life is three years.

CuT220B : This device is known to have two solid copper sleeves instead of a copper wire. The use of copper sleeves reduces the pregnancy rate. Its effective life is three years. (Figure 7)

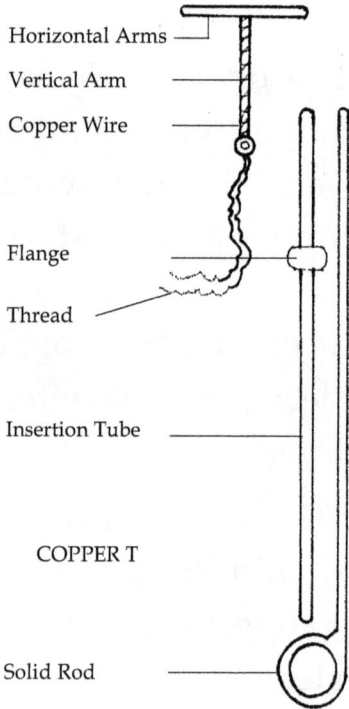

Fig. 7 Copper T 200B

Tcu-380 Ag: This device has three sleeves of solid copper and a coil of copper wire with the core of silver around the stem. The silver core is considered advantageous because it keeps the copper from fragmenting. Its effective life is four years.

Nova Tcu-200 A: This device has a silver leaf in the copper wire to prevent its fragmentation. Its effective life is three years. (Figure 8)

Medicated Devices: These are still under clinical trial. The currently available medicated device is progestasert. Incidentally, the use of this device is being discouraged

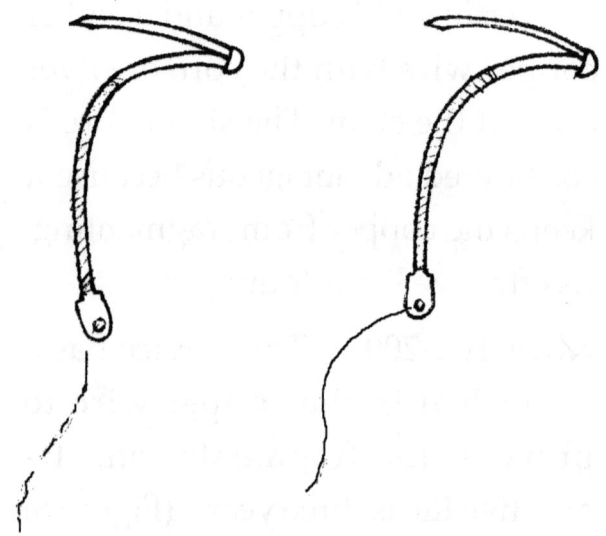

Fig. 8 Gravigard Copper 7 and CU7 or Nova Tcu-200A

because of its association with ectopic pregnancy. Currently, several other devices containing different doses of progestogen are under trial.

Millions of women throughout the world have used these devices because they found them effective, safe and convenient. Worldwide, more than 106 million women are using IUDs and their highest use is in developing countries, including Vietnam and China, where 30 per cent of married women in the reproductive age are using IUDs.

As of now, little is known about the concrete mechanism of the action of IUD. However, current literature shows • that all IUDs cause an inflammatory reaction in the endometrium so that phagocyte leucocyte may engulf the sperm or fertilized ovum; • that copper devices in particular alter the enzyme and trace element context of the endometrium (copper is spermicidal) and • that steroid releasing IUDs suppress the endometrium more or less like the progestrone-only pill. Further research is being carried out.

Are there specific conditions for the insertion of an IUD?
Basically, an IUD can be inserted at any time during the menstrual cycle. An IUD can also be inserted

immediately after the delivery of the placenta or at the time of a caesarian section, and at any time during the first seven days after abortion. In an IUCD insertion, the age factor is of no consequence - there is no minimum or maximum age for the use of an IUD.

Should an IUCD be inserted by a trained doctor/service provider only?

Yes, a woman can get an IUCD inserted by a trained doctor/service provider after careful gynaecological examination, anytime during her menstrual cycle, provided she is sure that she is not pregnant. She may prefer to get the IUD inserted midway through the menstrual cycle as at this stage the mouth of the cervix is a little wider. As mentioned before, a woman can get the IUD inserted at any age as long as she is sure that she is free from the risk of sexually transmitted disease. However, the IUD should be removed, at least one year after a woman's last menstrual cycle, when she reaches menopause.

Even a lactating woman who has not yet got her periods after delivery, can get an IUD inserted after ensuring that she is not pregnant. At present, IUDs are available free of cost in most health and family welfare centres all over the country.

How effective are IUDs and what are their advantages?

IUDs are highly effective. With most IUDs, pregnancy rates range from less than 1 to 3 per 100 women per year. The three most effective and widely used IUDs are - Tcu 380A, Tcu 200C, and MLCu-375. In many settings, continuation rates of these IUDs are quite high. Thus, next to oral contraceptives, the IUDs are highly effective. IUD expulsion rates have varied from less than one to more than seven per 100 women in the first year of use. Several factors have influenced expulsion of IUDs. However, there is a greater likelihood of expulsion of IUDs in the case of younger women and women who had never been pregnant or never had any children.

In terms of advantages, an IUD is one of the most effective and safe contraceptives. Its strength lies in the fact that it is convenient to use, for once it is inserted, it can provide protection for three to five years. Thus, healthy women wanting to postpone their next pregnancy can find it as their method of choice. It requires just one time motivation. Moreover it is free from the systemic effect of oral contraceptives. Also, there is prompt return to fertility after removal, and the user is at minimal risk of mortality.

What are the common side-effects of IUD and how can these be managed?
The common side-effects associated with IUDs are:

- Mild abdominal cramps or backache after insertion or at the time of periods.
- Increased menstrual bleeding, often with pain, during the first two to three months. However, lower rates of removal due to

bleeding and pain have been reported among older women or women with children. Hormone-releasing devices are known to decrease blood flow (LNG 20). These hormone-releasing IUDs may even protect against anemia; and

- Rare complications such as perforation of the uterus, infertility and ectopic pregnancy. Perforation of the uterus resulting from IUD insertion can be reduced by careful insertion techniques. Perforation may often go unnoticed at the time of insertion. If perforation is noticed during insertion, the IUD should be removed.

It would be better if the user is checked by a doctor/trained service provider after one month, and later, at least once in six months. But prompt medical attention should be sought in case of heavy bleeding, expulsion of the device, absence of monthly periods, or the absence of feeling of the string of the IUD. Complication rates of the IUD may vary even with the same IUD, from clinic to clinic, depending on a variety of factors, including a woman's age, parity and quality of care. The quality of care provided to the user can influence the continuation rate of an IUD. Training and experience of the service provider with regard to insertion techniques and management of initial side-effects are important factors. Properly trained service providers can help a great deal in reducing rates of removal of IUDs due to these side-effects and complications.

What are the conditions under which women should not get IUDs inserted?

Women with certain conditions should not get an IUD inserted. These are:

- If she is suspected to be pregnant;
- If she has irregular or heavy unexplained vaginal bleeding;
- If she has uterine fibroids or pelvic inflammatory disease;
- If she has maligancy of the genital tract; and
- If she has any history of ectopic pregnancy.

Can a woman use an IUD if she never had a baby or after she had a baby or after abortion or miscarriage?

Firstly, an IUD is not considered as the best method of contraception for a woman who never had a baby.

This is because the uterus of a woman who never had children is too small for an IUD. Secondly, a woman should have no problem in getting the IUD inserted just after she has a baby. A trained person can insert the IUD after vaginal delivery or through the abdominal incision after a caesarian section. Thirdly, a woman can also get an IUD inserted just after an abortion or a miscarriage, provided she does not have pelvic infection. But she should get the IUD inserted from a trained person, especially following a miscarriage, after sixteen weeks of gestation.

Is it necessary for a woman to receive antibiotics to prevent infection before an IUD insertion?

Generally, if a woman is healthy and the IUD insertion is done correctly, she would not need any antibiotics. Careful screening can help in avoiding the use of antibiotics. Current evidence suggests that antibiotics do not significantly reduce the risk of pelvic inflammatory disease.

Can a woman have babies after the removal of an IUD?

Normally, a woman can become pregnant after the removal of an

IUD. However, she has to understand that the IUD provides no protection against sexually transmitted diseases and that the IUD may even increase the chances of getting pelvic inflammatory diseases if she gets sexually transmitted diseases (STDs). These infections/diseases could even lead to infertility. She can take care of all these problems provided she has sex only with her husband who is uninfected.

Can an IUD cause discomfort to a woman's husband during sex and if so, should she seek replacement of the IUD?

A woman's husband may feel some discomfort only if the IUD has started to come out of the cervix. In such a situation, the best approach would be to seek medical attention. Regarding replacement of the IUD, she should consult the service provider. The commonly available IUDs are generally effective for three to four years.

Is there any possibility of the IUD travelling to any vital part of a woman's body?

Normally, the IUD remains within the uterus. However, in very rare cases it does pass through the wall of the uterus and rest in the abdomen. This may be attributable to some flaw during insertion and not to any slow movement through the wall of the uterus. There is no chance of the IUD travelling to any vital part of the body.

Is it safe for a diabetic woman to have an IUD?

Normally, a diabetic woman should not have any problem with an IUD. However, she must understand that she is at a greater risk of many infections which she may erroneously attribute to an IUD. In such situations, the best approach would be to seek consultation with a qualified doctor. She may not, on her own, be able to recognise signs and symptoms of sexually transmitted diseases. and so should seek medical attention in such situations.

Injectable Contraceptives And Norplant Implants

What are injectable contraceptives? What are their formulations and mode of action?

Injectable contraceptives are injected intramuscularly. Their compounds are slowly released in the blood circulation system to provide long-lasting hormonal activity. Injectable contraceptives have been introduced after the oral hormonal contraceptives. Their clinical trials were conducted in the

1960s. Way back in 1963, the Upjohn Company had begun clinical trials of medroxyprogesterone accetate injections (DMPA: Depo-Provera). Earlier in 1957, Schering AG had begun trials of norethisterone Oenanthate (NETOEN). While DMPA - Depo-Provera provides three months of protection, NETEN, commonly known as Noristerat, is effective only for two months. In the light of recent research by the WHO, and approval of DMPA by the United States Food and Drug Administration in 1992, the USAID may offer DMPA to various developing countries, for introducing it in their national family planning programmes. Worldwide, an estimated 30 million women have used injectable contraceptives and over six million are using them at present. Until recently, both DMPA and NETOEN were only licensed for short-term use. When properly used, injectable hormonal contraceptives are among the most effective methods of contraception.

It may be clarified that NETEN is prepared in an oily solution and, after injection, is hydrolysed to the biologically active steroid northisterone (NET). But the DMPA is formulated as a microcrystalline suspension of known particle size and the medroxy progesterone acetate, is released into the circulation and is itself biologically active. Injectables (DMPA and NET-EN) act mainly by inhibting ovulation, increasing the viscosity of the cervical secretions, thus forming a barrier to spermatozoa, changing the rate of ovum transport through the fallopian tubes, and making the endometrium less suitable for implantation.

Thus injectable contraceptives - both DMPA and NET-EN — offer several advantages as a method of contraception and are also acceptable to many women. In Thailand and Indonesia, where injectables are offered in the national family planning programmes, 12 per cent to 15 per cent of married women of reproductive age are relying on injectables.

For how long does an injectable work and how effective are they?

As injectables work mainly by preventing ovulation, they are highly effective. It has been recommended that 150 mg (3ml) DMPA (Depot medroxyprogesterone acetate) should be given within the first five days of the menstrual cycle and should be repeated after every 90 days (or 12 weeks). Some other regimens have also been tried (250 mg every 16 weeks, and 450 mg every 24 weeks) and reportedly they have a higher continuation rate. The pregnancy rate is reported to be 0.0-1.2 per 100 woman years with 150 mg every 12 weeks and 0.49 per 100 woman years with 450 mg every 24 weeks.

In case of NETOEN (Norethisterone Oenanthate) 200 mg (1ml) should be given within the first five days of the menstrual cycle and repeated after every 8 weeks for the first 6 months and thereafter at 12 weekly intervals. The pregnancy rate is reported to be 0.01 to 1.3 per 100 women years with 200 mg for 8-12 weeks. It may be emphasised that the effectiveness of the injectables also depends on the timing of the first injection, adherence to the injection schedule and the injection technique.

The dosages and the injection schedules ensure that the user can come even a little late for the next injection without risking pregnancy. A user of DMPA can get an injection up to two weeks late and possibly up to 4 weeks late. However, a user of NETEN can get an injection upto 1 week late and possibly upto 2 weeks and for monthly injections, upto 3 days late. But women experiencing spontaneous or induced abortion can get the first injection within the next 7 days.

If a woman wants to conceive after the use of injectables, she has to wait for six to eight months as injectables remain in the blood stream for several months. So far, there is no evidence that injectables cause infertility. There is also no difference in the time of return to fertility between long-term and short-term users of DMPA. However, amenorrhea may persist for several months after discontinuation of injectables.

Under what circumstances should women use injectable contraceptives?

Basically, injectable contraceptives are useful for couples who have completed their family and are not ready to accept a permanent method of family planning. But injectables are also useful for women planning birth control for more than two to three years. Even breastfeeding women in need of using hormonal contraceptives can use DMPA or NETEN. Injectables are also suitable for women who require maximum protection following immunization against rubella, for partners of men undergoing vasectomy, postpartum women awaiting sterilisation and for women in whom oestrogens are contraindicated and maximum protection is required. They are also useful for unreliable pill takers (for whatever reason including forgetfullness, etc.). Regarding their effectiveness, injectables are highly effective and reversible.

Name some of the advantages & disadvantages of injectable contraceptives?

Advantages of Injectables

- They can be administered by a private service provider and at one's own convenience.
- Injectables may increase production of prolactin suitable for lactating women.
- Amenorrhoea may be medically advantageous, particularly in a woman with iron-deficiency anaemia.
- Injectables reduce the risk of ovarian cancer by preventing

ovulation and also the risk of endometrial cancer.

- Injectables not only prevent unintended pregnancy but also protect a woman against ectopic pregnancy which can kill her from sudden and severe internal bleeding, if a fallopian tube ruptures.
- Injectables may also prevent pelvic inflammatary disease (PID) by thickening the cervical mucus and preventing STD from passing through the cervix.

Disadvantages of Injectables

- The changes in menstrual cycle and amenorrhea are the most common side effects of injectables. They are one of the main reasons for their discontinuation.

- With the use of DMPA, bleeding may be frequent and irregular, although it is not usually heavy. But with the use of NETEN, the return of regular menstruation is probably quicker than the DMPA.
- Most users of injectables gain weight, but this weight increase is almost certainly due to increased appetite and is not associated with fluid retention.

- Some users may experience breast tenderness and heaviness. There is a delay in return to fertility. Women may have to wait for 6 to 8 months and sometimes upto 2 years. Galactorrhoea may occur in those who are not breastfeeding.
- Availability of health personnel for providing injections at two or three monthly intervals may be difficult in certain settings.
- Headache, dizziness, changes in mood and loss of libido have also been reported.

But there is no reliable evidence showing that the incidence of these side-effects are higher than use of other forms of contraceptives

What factors influence acceptance of injectable contraceptives?

A variety of factors affect the availability and acceptability of injectable contraceptives. For instance, factors such as a previous experience of pregnancy may influence their decision to use contraception for family spacing or limitation. The user's contraceptive history may also influence acceptance of injectable contraceptives. Apart from these, other factors such as a woman's education, occupation and financial status may also influence her decision about accepting injectable contraceptives.

The user's own perception of the method's advantages and disadvantages can greatly influence her decision about accepting injectable contraceptives.

Injectable contraceptives are highly effective, reversible and are relatively long lasting. Their major disadvantages, such as the probability of irregular bleeding may be overcome through proper medical attention.

Acceptance of injectable contraceptives also depends considerably on the commitment of the service provider. There are a variety of health personnel engaged in providing injectable contraceptives to their clients in different settings. They need to be thoroughly informed about their advantages, disadvantages, side-effects and also non-contraceptive benefits. Their own beliefs and attitudes too can have an enormous effect on the acceptance of injectable contraceptives by the prospective clients. Thus, the trainers in the departments of obstetrics and gynaecology, paediatrics, community medicine, maternal and child health and other related departments need to ensure that all service providers are properly trained and capable of helping clients to manage their side-effects. The attitude of service providers will influence both method acceptance and continuation of use. It is crucial that they acquire knowledge and communication skills to respond convincingly to the queries of their clients. This can be possible only when the service providers are well-versed with the characteristics of the other contraceptive methods.

Certain cultural and religious factors may also influence the acceptance of contraceptive injectables. In cultures where drugs by injection is more acceptable than taking drugs by mouth, injectable contraceptives may be favoured. Women representing such cultural settings may find injectable contraceptives to be highly satisfactory. A client's overall decision about acceptance and use of a contraceptive method is influenced by factors such as side-effects the effectiveness, safety and cultural acceptability of the method. Non-acceptance of these injections is attributed to, weight gain in some women, feelings of bloatedness and breast tenderness, headaches, mood changes, loss of libido and delay in return of fertility. But the mode of its administration, the frequency of administration, the possibility of its reversibility and the cost of the method are considered as its positive attributes.

What are Norplant implants and at what stage should they be inserted?
Contraceptive Norplant implants are hormone releasing devices

which are made of synthetic material known as polymethylsiloxane. Implants are inserted into the subcutaneous tissue of the woman in specific areas. Under local anesthesia, the implants are placed under the skin of the arm within 10 to 15 minutes. Implants are available in the form of hollow capsules or solid rods impregnated with the hormone. Most rods and capsules are 2 to 4 cm long with an outside diameter of 2.4 mm. Implants may contain synthetic progestins commonly known as levonorgestrel, norgestrienone or ST 1435.

Levonorgestrel is highly effective. There are six capsules in a Norplant, each capsule containing 36 mg of levonorgestrel. It has been reported that in the first few weeks of use, the implants release 68 mcgs of levonorgestrel per day and the amount drops to 40 micrograms per day by the end of the first year of use, and to 30 micrograms by the end of the fifth year of use. The estimated effective life of a Norplant is at least five years. A three-year pregnancy rate is between 0.7 to 1 per 100 women. Women can get Norplant implants inserted anytime within seven days of her menstrual cycle or when she is reasonably sure that she is not pregnant. In case a woman is getting the implant inserted while she is menstruating there is no need to use a back-up method. But if she is not menstruating but getting it inserted on the 7th day, then a back-up method is needed for one week (or abstinence). The breast-feeding woman should wait at-least for six weeks before a Norplant insertion. Insertion of the Norplant implant is done by a trained service provider after following basic infection prevention measures.

For whom is a Norplant implant suitable? Can these cause cancer or ovarian cysts?

Firstly, regardless of age, all women can use Norplant implants. Even heavy women can use Norplant implants. They may or may not have children. Secondly, there is no evidence indicating that the implants can cause cancer. On the contrary, they may help to prevent endometerium cancer. But the possibility of a woman using Norplant implants having ovarian cysts is very much there, though most cysts disappear on their own without surgery. A woman using

Norplant implants should therefore be in touch with a service provider to get herself examined periodically.

Can a woman use Norplant implants for more than five years? How often should she return to the clinic for a follow-up?

There is no danger involved if Norplant implants are left in for more than five years. But leaving them in is not recommended. Norplant implants become less effective after five years and there may be a risk of ectopic pregnancy. Secondly, there is no need for a woman using Norplant implants to undertake periodic visits for a follow-up, unless she has specific problems. Even annual visits are not required for a woman using Norplant implants. She needs to visit the clinic only if she wants to have her capsules removed before five years.

Can a woman using Norplant implants continue her work immediately after insertion? Can implants break?

Firstly, a woman with a Norplant Implant can continue doing her usual work immediately after insertion. However, she should not bump the insertion site and should avoid getting it wet. It would be best if she could keep the insertion site dry and clean for atleast forty eight hours. Secondly, there is no chance for the capsules to break. They are flexible and under normal circumstances, there is no possibility of their breaking under the skin.

Oral Contraceptives

How popular are oral contraceptives?

Oral contraceptive are tablets or capsule to be taken orally. Oral contraceptives have already become the most popular method of family planning in many countries. Though oral contraceptives were introduced in the 1960s, more than 150 million women around the world, are now relying on them. Today, oral contraceptives - popularly known as "the pill", are considered to be the most effective and reversible form of contraception. It can be supplied to the users even by a well-trained non-physician.

How did oral contraceptives originate?

Way back in 1921, Haberlandt was the first scientist to indicate that the extract from the ovaries of pregnant animals could be used as oral contraceptives. Later, in 1937, Kurzrok, during treatment of dysmenorrhoea, noted that the ovarian oestrone was responsible for inhibiting ovulation and thus he felt that this hormone might be of value in fertility control. Later in the 1950s, when potent, orally active progestogens, became available, we could have oral contraceptive pills. These pills contained only progestogen and were effective in controlling the menstrual cycle. In 1956, Puerto Rico successfully introduced oestrogen and combined pill-Enovid in their national programme (norethynodrel plus mestranol). In America, the pill was approved in 1959, while in Britain, it was approved two years later. In 1959, when cardiovascular problems related to the dose of oestrogen came to light, the composition of the pill had to be changed markedly. In order to avoid the metabolic side-effects of oestrogen, progestogen–only pills were introduced in 1960, using derivatives of 19-nortestosterone and 17-acetoxyprogesterone. It has been reported that initially the dose of ethinyl estradiol in combination pills was 50 ug and when complications were noted its dose was reduced to 30 ug. Later, the dose of ethinyl estradiol was reduced to only 20 ug. Worldwide, combined pills are most frequently used today. Now a number of new oral combination contraceptive pills are available. They either contain newer progestins like gestodene norgestimate, desogestrel, or an even lower dose of estrogen as compared to 30 microgram pills. Most women can be effectively protected from pregnancy with a minimum amount of contraceptive hormones and both the 1/50 and the low-dose pills are excellent preparations for almost all women who do not have contraindications.

Name the oral contraceptives available in India? How helpful are they?

In India, one can get Mala-N free of charge from various health centres and family welfare centres. But one can get it even from the chemist's shops at a highly subsidized price.

Regarding their mode of action, the contraceptive combined pills mainly act in two ways: • by altering the neuro-endocrinal feedback system that controls the hypothalmic-pituitary ovarian relationship and • by inducing changes in the reproductive tract including the cervical mucus, the endometrium, the myometrium and the tubes. Because of multiple modes of action, contraceptive oral pills are considered to be highly effective. Even if ovulation takes place, pregnancy rarely occurs, since conditions in the reproductive tract are unfavourable for sperm and ovum transport and for implantation. The pills, therefore, are 99 per cent effective. A woman is fully protected as soon as she starts taking pills, unless her cycles are of 21 days or shorter. In such cases the woman should take additional precautions during the first 14 days of the first cycle only. You should know that certain drugs including amidopyrine, rifampicin, phenobarbitone, chlordiazepoxide, chlorpromazine meprobamate, ampicillin and dihydroergotamine reduce the effectiveness of oral pills. Thus you should consult your doctor before taking any of these drugs along with the pill.

What do you know about the availability and use of Mala-N?

Young women wishing to postpone their first pregnancy may like to use oral pills (Mala N is a popular Indian brand) as their method of choice. In the Indian market, easy availability of Mala N is a plus factor. Each packet of Mala N contains 28 pills (21 white pills containing hormones and 7 red pills). One can get Mala N free of charge from various health and family welfare centres, as it is included in the national family planning programme. One can even get it from a chemist's at a highly subsidized rate. If used correctly, Mala N is almost 100 per cent effective in preventing pregnancy. It is advantageous because the user will have regular periods with less bleeding and no pain during the periods. Another advantage is that Mala N can be used for five years without any break. If the user wants to become pregnant, all she needs to do is to stop taking the pills.

When and how often should a woman take the pill?

Regarding instructions, a woman should start taking the first pill on the first day of her menstrual cycle and she should continuously take one tablet a day. A woman should not stop taking the tablet during her menses. If a woman misses one pill on a particular day, she should take two pills the next day. But if she misses more than two pills, she should discontinue taking the pills and should rely on back-up methods till she gets her periods.

Regarding Mala N, the user must start taking Mala N from the fifth day of the menstrual period. She should form the habit of taking it at a particular time of the day on a regular basis - first taking the white pill, one each for twenty-one days, and then, taking the orange pill for each of the remaining seven days. One must ensure that there is no interruption in taking the pill. And it would be helpful if the user keeps with her an extra packet of the pills to maintain regularity. Missing a pill should not be taken lightly.

How long can a woman take the pill? Can it make her sterile or cause cancer or deformed babies?

Firstly, oral contraceptives can be used by most women of all ages until menopause. Women who smoke and who are above thirty-five and older should not use combined oral contraceptives. Secondly, the pill does not make a woman sterile and women who are taking the pill will be able to get pregnant when they stop taking it. They only have to wait for a few months for the return of their normal menstrual periods. Thirdly, there is no evidence showing that combined oral contraceptives can cause any common cancer. Some studies have indicated a certain linkage between breast and cervical cancer with the use of oral contraceptives. But then other studies have gone against these findings. Thus, current research does not show any linkage between combined oral contraceptives and cancer. Fourthly, there is no evidence showing that a child conceived after a woman stops taking oral contraceptives, will be deformed because of the pill.

Does a woman require pelvic examination before using the oral pill? Can the pill make her weak?

Pelvic examination is not a necessary condition for a woman who wants to start taking oral contraceptives. But in case, she has a gynaecological problem, pelvic examination might help her to know the reason. There is no evidence indicating that the pill could make a woman weak. On the contrary, using a pill may prevent anaemia. This is because women who use the pill lose much less menstrual blood than other women. But if she psychologically feels herself to be weak, she may seek medical attention. She need not stop taking the pill on her own as this will not protect her from getting pregnant. So, continuity of taking the pill is necessary for avoiding unplanned pregnancies.

Is it safe for a lactating woman to use oral contraceptives?

It is recommended that a lactating woman should avoid using oral contraceptives at least for six to eight weeks. Then, if she decides to use hormonal contraceptives, she should take progestin-only pills. These pills are considered safe for both the mother and her baby as these contain very little hormone. The user should take one pill a day at any time of the day. Women who are not breast-feeding can start taking oral contraceptives from the second to third week after delivery. The pill should be taken at the same time each day. A woman who is breast-feeding can continue with progestin-only pills, even if she stops breast-feeding, as these pills are very effective if used correctly and consistently. She should continue taking a pill at the same time every day, preferably late afternoon or 4 to 5 hours before sexual activity so that the pill's effect on the cervical mucus is maximum. Women who are breast-feeding and who are using progestin-only pills, should not shift to combined oral contraceptives or any other method containing estrogen until at least 6 months post-partum, as even low-dose estrogen in combined oral pills may decrease breast milk. Non - hormonal contraceptives methods can also be used.

What are the advantages and disadvantages of oral contraceptives?

Regarding advantages, combined oral contraceptives are considered 99 per cent effective in preventing pregnancy, if used properly. Oral contraceptives also minimize menstrual cramps and may help to reduce painful menstruation (dysmenorrhea). In addition, the pill generally reduces the number of days of menstrual flow. Thus there is reduction in the total amount of blood loss and intensity of flow during menstruation. The pill also produces regular menstrual periods and may be used for symptomatic control of bleeding patterns. And, women having iron deficiency, anemia, can be benefited, as menstrual blood loss is reduced to one half on an average, in case of pill users. Besides, pill users are relieved from pre-menstrual tension, anxiety or depression. The pills can be supplied by a well trained non-physician. Also, the risk of ovarian cysts and ovarian cancer is less among pill users. Oral contraceptives also reduce ovulatory pain (mittleschmerz) and are often used for the treatment or prevention of some forms of endometriosis. Thus pill users are also less likely to develop benign (non-cancerous) tumors of the breast than non-users of the pill. There is no risk of an ectopic pregnancy for pill users as is in the case of the IUD. Some studies have reported that the incidence of rheumatoid arthritis in pill users was half of that in non-users.

Regarding their disadvantages, some women may experience some side-effects with varying degrees of intensity. During the initial two to three months of pill taking, certain side-effects such as nausea and occasional vomiting and break-through bleeding or spotting may be experienced. These symptoms are not unusual or serious and diminish rapidly after three cycles of pill taking. But if these symptoms become intolerable for a user, she should stop taking the pills after consulting the service provider. Mild intermenstrual spotting during the first several cycles of pill taking is common. If this problem persists, the pills should be changed with pills having higher estrogen. Some women may experience scant menstruation or even amenorrhea (no menstruation) If continuous scant menstruation is disturbing her, she can change the regimen from a low-dose to a 1/50 pill or to a pill containing norgestrel after consulting her service provider.

Some women may have increased vaginal discharge while

taking the pill. Such women should seek medical attention. Some women may experience an increased facial skin pigmentation known as chloasma. This condition can be treated by using a vanishing cream. But they should seek medical attention. Some other symptoms which are not attributable directly to pill taking include, headache, depression, breast pain (mastalgia), weight changes and bloating, and loss of sex drive (libido). Though these are often attributed to pill taking, no definite statistical association with the pill use has been found.

Other rare but potentially serious conditions include: thrombphlebitis, thromboembolism, stroke, subarachnoid hemorrhage, heart attack, hypertension, benign liver tumors and gallstones. The incidence of these diseases varies significantly according to the pill user's age and other risk factors, including cigarette smoking. Thus any possible risk should be weighed against multiple benefits of pill use.

The users of the pill may experience certain minor discomforts such as headache, nausea, tenderness of breast and spotting between periods. These symptoms may be of a shorter duration during the first two-three months of use and may disappear without any treatment. In some cases, particularly in women over 35 years of age and who are smokers, there may be an increased risk of high blood pressure, heart attack and venous thrombosis. But major complications are very rare among pill users. Apart from regular medical check-ups, the user may seek medical attention and advice if she does not get her periods in two consecutive cycles and if the above side effects persist or if there is tightness in the chest or disturbance of vision.

What should be done if a woman forgets to take the pill?

Oral contraceptives are only as effective as the ability of the woman to remember taking them regularly. Forgetfulness on her part may lead to pregnancy. A woman should fix-up the time herself for taking the pill every day. If she forgets to take the pill, she should take two pills on the next day at the same time. The pill-taking should be made part of an already existing habit such as the evening meal or preparing for bed. Innovative methods for remembering to take the pill need to be developed.

Because of disturbance in the dose pattern, a woman may experience slight breakthrough bleeding or nausea. But if she misses three pills, the chances of her becoming pregnant increases, and she should use another form of contraception immediately. A study has reported that the risk of pregnancy increases when the pill is missed around the beginning or end of the cycle and not in mid cycle.

What are the contraindications for the users of oral contraceptives?

Oral contraceptives are not recommended for women who are pregnant, or who have irregular, unexplained vaginal bleeding, diabetes, jaundice during pregnancy or in the last six months, any disease affecting the liver or gall bladder, suspected or confirmed cancer of any organ, a heart problem or venous thrombosis, rifampcin therapy (Anti-tuberculosis treatment), severe headache (focal migrane), severe allergy, epilepsy and addiction to smoking.

What are emergency contraceptive pills and how should they be used?
These are pills which should be used by a woman within 72 hours of unprotected intercourse. The

purpose is to protect the woman by delaying or preventing ovulation. Generally, women experience nausea and vomiting after using these pills. It is recommended that combined oral contraceptives containing 50 ug ethinyl estradoil and 250 ug levonorgestorel, should be taken in each dose. Two doses are recommended to be taken 12 hours apart and preferably within 72 hours. If pills containing 30 ug ethinyl estradial and 150 ug levonorgestrel are used, then four tablets should be taken followed by another four, 12 hours later. It is better if a woman can be provided with these tablets in advance when she visits the service provider. Providing information and supplies in advance can be convenient to a woman as it will save her another visit to the clinic and she will be able to take the pills within 72 hours after unprotected sex.

Sterilisation

Female Sterilisation

How is female sterilisation accomplished?

Basically, female sterilisation is accomplished by surgically occluding the fallopian tubes so that the egg and the sperm cannot meet. The methods used for female sterilisation vary according to the surgical approach used to reach the tubes, the timings of the procedure and the procedure used to occlude the tubes. Surgeons can approach the fallopian tubes either through the abdomen or through the vaginal cul-de-sac. The abdominal approach is the most common. Two techniques used are laparoscopy and minilaparotomy. But this approach is also used in regular laprotomy. In the vaginal approach, the two techniques used are colpotomy and culdoscopy. Each approach is further subdivided for using an endoscope. There are various ways to occlude the fallopian tubes so as to make them incapable of transporting the ovum and preventing the spermatozoa access. The methods of occlusion are: tubaligation; silastic ring;

plastic clip; electrocoagulation and removal of tubes, ovaries, uterus. (Salpingactomy, oophorectomy and hysterectomy). Laparoscopy is becoming the most popular approach to female sterilisation both in developing and developed countries. It can be safely performed using local anesthesia. Laparoscopy is performed by a trained gynecologist with sophisticated equipment - the laparoscope. The entire procedure takes about half an hour. Within 5-6 hours, a woman can return home. It does not require hospitalization. In fact, a woman can resume her normal duties the next day. However, she should refrain from intercourse at least for three weeks.

How popular is female sterilisation?

The introduction of the laparoscopic technique has increased the popularity of female sterilisation. This procedure is easier and less time-consuming. The acceptance of female sterilisation has increased considerably during the past two and a half decades. Nearly 60 per cent of Indian couples using contraception are protected by female sterilisation. Female sterilisation is also widely used in other Asian countries including Bangladesh, Fiji, Nepal, Sri Lanka, Taiwan, Thailand and the Philippines. Over a decade ago, its prevalence was highest in South Korea - 37 per cent of married couples in the reproductive age were relying on female sterilisation. In China, 30 per cent of married women - 63 million - were relying on female sterilisation. The main reason for higher acceptance of female sterilisation in many countries was the support given to it by the government. In some Latin American countries, despite age and parity restrictions, female sterilisation has become quite widespread. The main reason for high acceptance of female sterilisation in these countries is women's desire for not having more children. In E1 Salvador, where the average reproductive age and parity is reported to be 28 and 3.5, high acceptance of sterilisation is responsible for continuing fertility decline. Here, 90 per cent of women have heard of voluntary sterilisation and they know where to get it. In Guatemala parity requirements are more relaxed. Sterilisation is legally permitted only to save the life of the woman and it must be performed by a physician in a hospital. A decade back, in the US female sterilisation was the most widely used method. Nearly one-fourth of married women in the reproductive age were sterlised for contraceptive reasons. In former West Germany too, a high prevalence of female sterilisation was reported. Of late, the demand for female sterilisation is on the increase in certain African countries including Ghana, Kenya, Nigeria, Tanzania and Zimbabwe, as these countries have incorporated female sterilisation into their national family planning programmes. The need for providing safe, effective and high quality care for women seeking voluntary sterilisation is likely to increase in the near future.

Are there different approaches to female sterilisation?

There are different approaches to female sterilisation. They are listed below:

Laparoscopic Sterilisation: This is the most common approach to female sterilisation. This procedure is simple and does not require any hospitalization. The woman is generally asked to report in the morning and she can go back home after 5-6 hours. She can resume normal activities within a day.

However, she should refrain from sex at least for three weeks. In case of non-absorable sutures or where clips are used to close the incision (incision is given below the naval), the woman will have to return after a week for removal. She can visit for a follow-up after consultation with the service provider. Some of the complications due to laparoscopy include, bleeding, uterine perforation, accidental burns and bowel trauma. But each of these complications occurs only in 1 per cent of all procedures. This procedure can be performed only by trained gyneacological surgeons and is highly effective with a very low mortality rate.

Minilaparotomy

Mini laparotomy (minilap) means entering the abdomen through a small incision and it depends on the use of a uterine elevator which is inducted into the uterine cavity through the cervix. Occlusion can be accomplished either with bands or clips or by ligation (tying and cutting). Certain contraindications to mini-laparotomy out-patients are: extreme obesity; pelvic pathology and serious illness. But complications of minilaparotomy are: bleeding; uterine perforations and bowel or bladder trauma.

Laparotomy

Laparotomy is the most commonly used method of female sterilisation among post-partum women (within 48 hours of delivery). The procedure requires 20-30 minutes and can be performed under a variety of anesthetic techniques. It is reported that during this period the uterus is enlarged and it is relatively easier to reach through the incision without elevation. Traditional laparotomy is not generally performed these days as the procedure requires 3-5 days of hospital stay and a lengthy postoperative recovery of 4-6 weeks. This technique is used only in women who go in for sterilisation due to pelvic adhesions or other pathological conditions or if surgical indications exist. This procedure is quite effective. But it has higher complications, including post-operative infection and bleeding.

Some clients seek reversal of sterilisation. There are diverse motivations for seeking a reversal of sterilisation. It has been estimated that two thirds of reversal requests come from clients whose marital status is changed. Yet the overall frequency of requests for this is very low. Varied success rates have been reported by specialists in sterilisation reversals. But success in reversing sterilisation is directly related to how much viable tubes remain.

Is it possible for a woman to have her sterilisation reversed and become pregnant again?

It needs to be thoroughly understood, that as of now, surgery to reverse sterilisation is a possibility in the case of those women who have enough tube left. But even in these cases, surgery may not always lead to a pregnancy.

Even when pregnancy occurs, the chances of ectopic pregnancy may increase. In any case, the procedure is not only difficult but also expensive. It is available only at few advanced centres. Thus, it would be good if a woman considers sterilisation as a permanent method right at the beginning. If she retains any desire for more children, she must seek other methods of family planning. If a woman becomes pregnant after sterilisation, she was probably already pregnant at the time of sterilisation.

Would it be better for a woman to have female sterilisation or have her husband undergo vasectomy?

Firstly, it would be better if the decision about sterilisation is taken jointly by each couple. Both the methods are very effective, safe and permanent, provided they are sure that they do not want to have any more children. Secondly, it would be necessary for the couples to know that vasectomy, as compared to female sterilisation, is simpler and safer to perform. It is not only less expensive but also slightly more effective (after the first three months). Thus, at least from medical considerations, vasectomy should be preferable. Finally, each couple must make a careful decision after taking into consideration all the pros and cons of male and female sterilisation.

What kind of information does a woman need before deciding about sterilisation for herself?

Firstly a woman should possess balanced information about female sterilisation as well as about other family planning methods so that she could take the right decision. Secondly, she must delay seeking sterilisation if she is pregnant, has serious post-partum or post-abortion complications, unexplained vaginal bleeding, pelvic inflammatory disease (PID), sexually transmitted diseases, acute heart disease, gall bladder disease, active viral hepatitis, severe iron deficiency, anemia, (hemoglobin less than 7g/dl), acute lung disease, gastroentritis, abdominal skin infection or any AIDS-related illness. Thirdly, she should be very careful in her decision-making about ending her fertility and finally, she should consult service providers for clarifications and, if possible, her female relatives and friends who have undergone sterilisation.

When can female sterilisation be performed and are there any contraindications?

Female sterilisation can be performed any time, provided the woman is sure that she is not pregnant. Post-partum women can also undergo sterilisation within the first seven days of delivery. Even a woman having a cesarean delivery can undergo sterilisation within seven days as long as she is stable. In a woman undergoing abortion, sterilisation can also be performed concurrently or within seven days post-abortion, if she has no infection. In the absence of complications, sterilisation can be performed at the time of abortion. But in breast-feeding women local anesthesia is preferred, as general anesthesia may affect lactation. Accordingly, female sterilisation should be provided by trained doctors and other health personnel with adequate surgical experience.

Regarding contraindications, a woman should not undergo sterilisation • if she has cardiorespiratory insufficiency; • if she is overweight; • if she has undergone any previous abdominal surgery; • if she is mentally ill; • if she is having bleeding disorders; • if she is having malignancy; • if she has severe nutritional deficiency such as hypoproteinemia, anemia, and vitamin deficiency; and • if she is suspected to be pregnant.

Women in general must have a thorough understanding of certain important features of sterilisation. They should be well informed and should know that it is a surgical procedure with a small risk of complications. They should be informed that though it is a reversible procedure, its reversibility cannot be guaranteed. There is a chance of failure.

Is there any additional information about sterilisation that can help a woman decide about it?

Firstly, a woman should know that sterilisation would not hurt her because she would receive local anesthesia to stop pain. She should also understand that laparoscopy may hurt less than mini laparoscopy. Besides, she must know that post-partum minilaparotomy (just after delivery) may even hurt less because it requires less moving of the uterus. Secondly, a woman should know that after sterilisation, she can have sex as usual. In fact, she may find sex better because she would not be worried about getting pregnant. Thirdly, sterilisation will neither make her slim nor fat. Fourthly, sterilisation will not change her monthly periods or stop menstrual bleeding. Only if she is using a hormonal method or IUD before insertion she may find a change in her menstrual bleeding pattern.

What are the advantages of female sterilisation and are there any complications associated with it?

Over the past two decades, we found a tremendous increase in the number of women undergoing voluntary sterilisation, both in developed and developing countries. Some of the reasons for its increased acceptance are given below: • women, both in rural and urban areas, find it an effective and convenient method to protect themselves from unwanted pregnancies; • sterilisation is a one-time procedure and requires no supplies and no further action, once the procedure is completed; • there are no long-term side-effects; • couples who want to limit their family size, at a younger age, to fewer children, may find it useful;

and • family planning has become a social norm among educated couples in many countries.

How effective are methods of tubal occlusion performed by laparoscopy in preventing pregnancy?

All methods of tubal occlusion performed by laparoscopy are over 99 per cent effective in preventing pregnancy. But occlusion by electro-coagulation is considered to be slightly more effective than occulusion by the ring or clip. Laparoscopy complications include: bleeding, uterine perforation, accidental burns, bowel trauma and major vessel perforation.

Complications occur slightly more frequently with electro-coagulation. But there is near total absence of infection as a result of laparoscopic sterilisation.

Are there any contraindications or complications in laparascopy sterilisation?

Major complications, such as anesthesia related injury, infection, hemorrhage and cardiovascular complications have been reported in about one per cent of the cases. But minor complications such as wound infection or slight bleeding have been reported in less than five per cent of the cases. In developed countries, such as the US, deaths due to female sterilisation were rare (13 deaths in about 9,00,000 cases in the US between 1978 and 1980), in other words, one in every 70,000 procedures. Worldwide, voluntary female sterilisation is the number one method of family planning. An estimated 138 million women are protected from unwanted pregnancy by voluntary female sterilisation. Female sterilisation is widespread, especially in Latin America, Asia and the US. There are reasons for this. Women find sterilisation an effective, convenient and safe way to protect themselves from unwanted pregnancies. Laparoscopy with local anesthesia has enhanced the availability of female sterilisation in many cultural settings.

Male Sterilisation

What is vasectomy?

Vasectomy (male sterilisation) is a permanent method of contraception for men involving a single surgical procedure. It is one of the simplest and most readily available forms of contraception. It is highly effective and requires 15-20 minutes to perform the surgical procedure under local anesthesia. For couples who definitely want no more children, it offers an alternative to female sterilisation.

Most vasectomies are done for contraceptive reasons, but during the early 1900s they were done mainly for non-contraceptive reasons. These were done mainly to cure urinary or prostatic diseases, to treat impotence, or alternatively, to lower the sex drive. Medical research has now demonstrated that vasectomy has no such effects.

What are the advantages and disadvantages of Male Sterilisation?

Advantages

It is a one-time surgery, requiring a specific procedure for 10-15 minutes. It is safe and effective. Moreover, there are no adverse effects on sexual performance or masculinity or on male hormonal balance. It is economical and is done under local anesthesia.

Disadvantages

It is not suitable for men who desire to have children in future because it is not easily reversible. Moreover, surgery is required. Some complications like bleeding and pain may occur. And some men may develop psychological problems related to sexual behaviour.

Vasectomies must be performed by trained health professionals. In

India most health centres have trained doctors to perform the procedure. If performed properly, vasectomy is a highly effective method. After surgery, the user is required to use another contraceptive method for some time (12 weeks). But vasectomised men can be at the risk of acquiring sexually transmitted diseases. Therefore they should use condoms to protect themselves and their partners.

Some of the post-operative short-term complications are: • pain and swelling around the incision; • seepage of blood under the skin where small vessels are ruptured; • postoperative infection around the incision; • haematoma - bleeding into the sactoral sac which can cause pain and infection; • granulomas — which are symptomless and respond to conservative treatment; though persistent and painful granulomas may require surgical intervention.

What is the historical background of vasectomy?

If you look into its history you will find that the first vasectomy was performed in 1832 by Cooper on his dog. But vasectomy is also mentioned in the ancient Hindu literature 'Atharvaveda'. Vasectomy became popular when, in 1883, Guyon reported that it caused atrophy of the prostate gland and reduced the incidence of post-prostatectomy epididmititis. In the early part of the century, followers of the Eugenics movement, erroneously believed that sterilisation, forced or voluntary, of men or women, with particular diseases and undesirable traits, could reduce the occurrence of such diseases or traits in future generations. In some countries at that time involuntary vasectomy was legalized for the feeble minded, for insane criminals and others who were viewed as unacceptable by society. This practice led to certain excesses and abuses. Now the use of involuntary vasectomy for eugenic purposes is illegal in nearly all societies. Vasectomy became popular between 1940 to 1960 as a permanent method of family planning. India, China, the United States of America and the United Kingdom had included it in their national family planning programmes. By the 1980s, vasectomy was also included in the national family planning programmes in many other countries. It became an important method of contraception in China, Nepal, Bangladesh, Sri Lanka and Thailand. However, vasectomy was less accepted in Brazil, Guatemala, the Philippines and some European countries. In fact, vasectomy became a major family planning method only in six developed countries - the US, New Zealand, Australia, Great Britain, Canada and the Netherland. However, among developing countries, vasectomy became more popular in China, India and South Korea. Some of the reasons for less acceptance of vasectomy by men are: fear of losing manhood and fear of the surgical procedure, thus putting all responsibility of family planning on women. Female sterilisation is more commonly accepted than male sterilisation. Worldwide, by the end of 1994, 42 million couples were relying on male sterilisation as compared to 140 million couples who were relying on female sterilisation. But now the trend is changing because of the introduction of the no-scalpel vasectomy.

What is the no-scalpel technique?
The no-scalpel technique was developed in China. It is almost

bloodless and it appears to reduce the incidence of complications from haematoma. The procedure is performed under local anesthesia. More than 10 million no-scalpel procedures have been performed in China. In other countries more doctors are getting training for this. In conventional vasectomy procedure, a 1-2 cm incision is made in the scrotal skin to expose the vas deferens and then each vas deferens is blocked by tying, cautery or clipping, to prevent passing of sperms. The complications with this procedure include bleeding, hematoma and infections.

Can vasectomy be offered only to men who have reached a certain age? Will it affect their health and sexual ability?

Regardless of age or the number of children, a man can undergo vasectomy. Vasectomy in modern times cannot be limited to any specific age group. The decision about vasectomy should be taken after possessing balanced information on all aspects related to it.

So far, there is no evidence indicating that vasectomy affects health by increasing risks of heart disease or cancer. A vasectomised man will find no change in his sexual ability and there will be no after-effect of vasectomy on his testicles, ejaculation of semen or erection.

Is it possible for a man to have his vasectomy repressed?

It is possible to reverse vasectomy through surgery though it may not always lead to pregnancy. Thus, from all considerations, vasectomy should be considered as a permanent method People desiring to have more children should seek alternative methods of contraception. Men may prefer vasectomy because it is relatively simpler and safer to perform. For medical reasons too, vasectomy is advisable.

How can one be sure that vasectomy is working?

In order to ensure that vasectomy is working, one has to resort to a microscopic examination of the sperm. A semen specimen can be collected either through masturbation or through a condom. The absence of sperms on it would prove that vasectomy is working. A vasectomised person can seek the help of a service provider for this purpose, as the facilities for microscopic examination of sperms in the semen are provided at various health centres and hospitals.

How effective is male sterilisation? Are there any reasons for its failure?
Vasectomy is considered as the most effective method of contraception. Pregnancy rates in this procedure are lower than in other methods of contraception. A failure rate of 0.1-0.5 per cent has been reported during the first year. It is difficult to assess the exact failure rate, as different techniques have been used in different studies. Some of the reasons responsible for the failure of vasectomy are: • unprotected intercourse during the 12 weeks after surgery; • when recanalization or rejoining of the vas is done within three to four months after

vasectomy; and • failure on the part of the service provider in identifying the vas at the time of operation.

What factors affect availability, accessibility and the acceptance of vasectomy?

A number of factors affect availability, accessibility and acceptance of vasectomy in different cultural settings. Availability of vasectomy itself is dependent on factors such as, favourable political climate, favourable laws and their legal interpretation, favourable religious influences, cultural beliefs and attitudes and professional interest. Accessibility includes:

- adequate resources for services;
- convenience of services;
- adequate information about services;
- an adequate referral system;
- adequate screening of the client; and
- affordability.

Factors affecting its acceptance include:
- knowledge about vasectomy;
- beliefs and attitudes about vasectomy;
- image of the vasectomy programme; and
- personal needs and motivations.

In some settings, remuneration or incentives have been provided for physicians to increase the acceptance of vasectomy. But good counselling can also help a man to decide about vasectomy.

Other Methods of Family Planning

Are there any post-coital methods of family planning? If so, are they effective?

Yes, there are several post-coital methods of family planning. Post-coital methods are used in cases of unplanned and unprotected intercourse, suspected contraceptive failure (caused by a broken condom, a dislodged diaphragm or a missed pill) and rape or incest. These should not be considered as regular family planning methods. They are intended for emergency use. In many cultural settings, people have relied on various indigenous types of post-coital methods to avoid conception. These include, violent body movements to expel semen, use of pepper post-coital pessaries and post-coital douches with substances like wine and garlic. Other substances used for post-coital douches include vinegar, alum, lemon juice and certain carbonated soft drinks. In medical circles, the most frequently used post-coital methods involve administration of steroids hormones (estrogens/progestogen combination) within 72 hours of unprotected intercourse. Estrogens prevents pregnancy by interfering with the implantation of the blastocyst in the endometerium, by altering the endometerial development.

There are various side-effects of estrogens such as nausea and vomiting. In some cases, spotting has also been recorded. A commonly used dose regimen consists of taking 0.1 mg of ethinylestradiol and 0.5mg of levonosgestrel soon after exposure and again 12 hours later. But regimens containing ethinylestradiol and norgestrel, danazol, levonorgestrel or norethisterone have also been used. Failure rates for the combined estrogen/progestrone treatment range from 0 to 2.5 per cent.

Other side effects are irregular uterine bleeding, breast tenderness and headache. Another post-coital family planning method is that a copper containing IUD can be inserted within five days of unprotected coitus. This is advantageous because the woman can be protected from an unwanted pregnancy as long as the device is effective. This is particularly suitable for women in whom steroids/hormones are contraindicated. But it is contraindicated in the case of multiparous women. Insertion of an IUD is not recommended in women with an undetected pregnancy, pelvic inflammatory disease or gonorrhea. Women receiving post-coital contraception would need to contact the service provider one month after administration to confirm the absence of pregnancy. This can help in adopting other preventive measures. In the absence of large- scale studies on post-coital insertion of IUCDs, it is difficult to assess adequately the failure rate. But method failure can prove disastrous and may result in an extra uterine pregnancy.

What types of contraceptives are suitable for lactating women?

Most women are infertile for four to eight weeks after delivery and this period could be prolonged up to two years if a woman continues to breastfeed. Besides, some role may also be played by factors such as maternal age, parity and nutritional status. Barrier contraceptives are particularly suitable in such cases since they have no effect on lactation or the quality of breast milk.

Condoms and spermicides may be used in the immediate post-partum period but the diaphragm cannot be properly fitted until the vaginal canal has returned to its normal size and shape. Lactating mothers would, therefore, need counselling about the use of appropriate contraceptive methods as soon as they resume sexual activity.

What contraceptive methods may be advisable for women in the late reproductive years?

Women who are in the late reproductive years may find their best contraceptive choice in the use of barrier methods and spermicides.

This is because many of them may have medical contraindications preventing the use of other methods such as hormonal methods or the IUDs. These women are likely to attach greater importance to convenience, quality of care and cost. Moreover, they may not like to go to the family planning clinics.

What is Medical Termination of Pregnancy (MTP) and what are its side effects?

Another name for Medical Termination of Pregnancy is abortion.

Abortion is on the increase in most countries due to rapid urbanization and economic development. The practice of abortion is as old as civilization itself. The first reference to cervical dilation was made in the fifth century B.C. But abortion was also practised in primitive societies. Several herbal remedies were used for this purpose. In ancient Greece, abortion was accepted as a permissible act by the expectant mother to get rid of her unwanted pregnancy. Hippocrates (460-380 BC) was not against abortion. But he was credited with having endorsed violent exercises as a means of disturbing conception. Abortion has been a controversial subject for decades. In the mid-thirteenth century, abortion was given the status of a legal offence, punishable under civil law in many countries but only if the foetus had already animated. The socialist countries of Eastern Europe had introduced liberal abortion laws during the last four decades. Most of these countries allowed abortion on request from a woman specially if the conception was of less than three months duration.

Before an abortion, a woman is tested for Rh factor, hemoglobin level, diabetes and other relevant conditions, including a cervical culture, for assessment of infection in the lower genital tract. In case of infection, she is treated before she is permitted to undergo an abortion.

Medical Termination of pregnancy can be performed under local, spinal or general anesthesia. Several technical options are available for terminating a pregnancy after the 12th week, but all have some disadvantages. Hysterectomy can be performed only if there are pathological conditions. A review of studies indicates a low mortality rate of women undergoing MTP if the abortion is performed before 12 weeks of pregnancy. The risk of mortality also decreases if appropriate techniques are applied by experienced service providers. An adequate follow-up is required during post-operative care. Normally, a woman is sent back home after 2-3 hours of the abortion, but she is advised to abstain from sexual intercourse for up to 2-3 weeks.

Some of the complications of MTP are: excessive bleeding, fever, severe cramps, pain, uterine perforation and nausea/vomiting during the procedure. But these can be managed with proper care. Lastly, women should not adopt abortion as a method of family planning, rather they should use other reliable methods of contraception. They should opt for an abortion only as a last resort.

What is the legal status of Medical Termination of Pregnancy (abortion) in India?

In India, the Medical Termination of Pregnancy (MTP) Act was passed in 1971. According to this, a woman can lawfully demand abortion. Under this act, an abortion can be performed on a woman only up to 20 completed weeks of pregnancy. MTP must be performed only by a qualified person having a postgraduate degree or diploma in obstetrics and gynecology. There must be adequate facilities like an operation theatre, oxygen, suction instruments, etc.

What is Lactational Amenorrhoea Method (LAM) and how effective is it?

LAM is a method of family planning based on the physiology of breast-feeding. Three criteria are used for determining the effectiveness of this method: • whether there is an absence of periods; • whether a woman is fully or nearly fully breast-feeding, i.e. breast-feeding an infant exclusively day and night and on demand of the infant; and • whether the period gap after delivery is six months (post partum). The risk of pregnancy in the first six months after childbirth is about 2 per cent. Women relying on LAM are at risk of STDs including HIV/AIDS. Therefore condoms or other barrier methods for STD protection should be used. The risk of pregnancy is higher after six months post-partum. Further research on the efficacy of the extended Lactational Amenorrhea Method is needed.